Is This the Night: Finding Inner Peace

A self-care guide for
family & friends impacted by a suicidal crisis

Annemarie Matulis

Also by Annemarie Matulis

Embracing Imperfection:
the healing journey of a suicide attempt survivor (2017)
with co-author Tracey Pacheco Medeiros

Documentaries

A Voice at the Table, 2014
https://vimeo.com/92330799
http://avoiceatthetable.org/index.html

Voices Still Unheard, 2016
https://vimeo.com/170810220

Voices from the Shadows, 2017

Acknowledgements

Is This the Night: Finding Inner Peace has been several years in development with multiple revisions. I am not being spiritually arrogant when I say that I am blessed to have so many wicked awesome people with whom I walk on this healing journey. There is no way I can list everyone, so I won't. I trust that you know who you are and that I am grateful for your encouragement and belief in my ability to be of service to others.

A huge and grateful thank you to the Spirit above, whom I do call God, for allowing me a second chance at life. Also on the gratitude list: Tracey Pacheco Medeiros for inviting me along on her healing path (however reluctantly) and for letting me borrow Ashes for my many self-care walks.

George Larkin without whom I wouldn't get to half the places I need to go. Tracey covers the other half.

The courageous people in our films, *A Voice at the Table*, *Voices Still Unheard*, and *Voices from the Shadows*. It was from those experiences that this workbook and the companion workshop evolved. I know how it feels to not fit in, to feel broken and alone. A loving thank you to those who circled around me so many years ago and helped me find my own quiet place in the light, and taught me to weave that hope and healing into a tapestry of inner peace.

Dr. Bart Andrews for having faith in my ability to provide support to the Zero Suicide Missouri/NAMI St. Louis family and friend project *Finding Help and Hope: Supporting Loved Ones Fighting Suicide* hosted at Mercy St. Louis and Mercy Jefferson with this workbook.

Most of all, this workbook is dedicated to the millions upon millions of family members and close friends of loved ones who have experienced a suicidal crisis of any kind. And when the smoke cleared and the dust settled, realized that there was absolutely nothing available to them as a healing resource. Nothing. There is now. This one's for you. With love, from one "family" to another.

In Memorium, a special thank you to Dr. Phil Rodgers for his guidance and encouragement. I had so hoped to hand deliver a copy to him. Much love, Phil. You are missed.

Contents

Preface

Is There a Need?

Throughout my life I've been involved in a number of organizations as an employee, consultant or volunteer. Many had a basic criteria that must be met before money is spent, a new program developed or action taken – *Is There a Need?*

So, the question related to this workbook and its companion workshop was, *"Is there a need?"*

Yes, there is. It boils down to the fact that millions of people are impacted by suicide every year. For some, it's the loss of a loved one to suicide. For others, it's the terrifying discovery that a loved one is contemplating suicide or has already made an attempt or several attempts.

"Will they make another attempt?" can linger in the dark recesses of our minds for a lifetime. And that's fear personified.

I've dedicated more than thirty years of my life to advocating for societal changes in how we address domestic violence. There was a need 30-35 years ago to bang the drum loudly for domestic violence, to write about it, to change laws, to create shelters, to change the clinical approach to victims and to educate law enforcement, the military and so many others about how to deal with all aspects of domestic violence. And yet prejudice and discrimination still worm their way into the public discussion about violence related to families and relationships. And still the violence continues.

At the same time, I became involved with supporting those struggling with alcohol and drug addiction. We've spent decades and billions on fighting alcoholism and drug addiction. And we're still not sure how well that worked out for this country.

Along the way, through an invitation from leaders in the Massachusetts Department of Public Health's Suicide Prevention Program, I began my journey into the field of suicide prevention.

We are blessed to have resources for loss survivors – those left behind by the death of a loved. We need much more. We are grateful that doors are being cracked open to recognize the value of the lived and learned experience and expertise of suicide attempt survivors. With that said, as you read this, there is next to nothing to help support friends and families of suicide attempt survivors to find their way free from the anxiety and stress, darkness and anger, frustration and a sense of helplessness…to find their way to the path of freedom from fear. That bothers me.

As a woman who survived brutal violence, I know their fear. The more I began to write this workbook and prepared to present the retreat workshop, the more I realized how much domestic violence victims have in common with friends and family of attempt survivors. And once I had that "light bulb" moment, the writing came swiftly but not easily. It meant taking an inward journey back to the nightmare, the pain and the suffering, things I've long since moved on from – but that's the point: perhaps I can share a little bit about how I *did* that and just maybe help others find that precious inner peace we all seek or at least to begin the journey. Because during this writing journey, I had another "light bulb" moment – I *am* the friend and family of a suicide attempt survivor. Equally important, I have joined forces with many other families and friends because no family or friend with a loved one who has struggled with a suicidal crisis should have to walk this path alone.

The Why Now?

The discussion about what more to do to support those in suicidal crisis – with a focus specifically on suicide attempt survivors began to stir a number of years ago. In 2014, there were some solid rumblings. The American Association of Suicidology (AAS) announced the formation of a new division at its conference: ASLE (Attempt Survivors/Lived Experience) and two weeks later, _A Voice at the Table_ was screened at the Massachusetts Conference for Suicide Prevention. The documentary is a call to action to bring the voices of suicide attempt survivors to all tables in the field of suicidology, or as Dr. Bart Andrews prefers, to the field of life-ology.

As the Executive Producer and Director of that documentary, a couple of other items evolved from that filming process. First, that those who have traveled further along a path to healing from a suicidal crisis were still seeking a safe haven to hang out in from time to time to do a sort of spiritual and emotional check-in. So I created a wellness check workshop series. Second, that there was absolutely no support mechanism for the family and friends of this particular group of people. People just like me. So I created a retreat workshop. In July of 2014, the National Action Alliance for Suicide Prevention published The Way Forward: Pathways to hope, recovery and wellness with insights from lived experience.

And my guess is you're sitting here wondering what the hell that has to do with your current situation. A lot. Most importantly, you are not alone the way I was about 20 years ago. No one should have to struggle through this fear and anxiety alone, with no compass to know which way to turn. The workshop series you are about to step into is not "the" answer, but experience has shown some folks and I that it sure helped us to get started. And don't forget to keep breathing.

Annemarie Matulis, October 2017

This project is an adaptation of a retreat workshop developed in 2013

Is This the Night: *traumatized by fear, finding inner peace*

Some ramblings about finding freedom from paralyzing fear…
Dedicated to the friends & families of suicide attempt survivors, this may also benefit suicide loss survivors, battered women, men who experienced violence as children or adults, veterans and their families, and anyone else terrorized by fear…

The workshop description at the 2016 Massachusetts Conference for Suicide Prevention program stated:

Is This the Night -Finding Inner Peace was designed for and dedicated to the family & friends of suicide attempt survivors in response to a recommendation in the National Action Alliance for Suicide Prevention's July 2014 *The Way Forward* to address "*coping strategies to avoid burnout, especially in consideration of their vigilance and help-giving efforts.*"

In New England, we hear the familiar preparation checklist whenever we brace for the winter blizzard or the nor'easter. Those who hope to keep us safe do their best to forewarn us as early as possible to avoid disasters. The check-list concept is a well-used tool to avoid disasters. *Is This the Night* weaves the wellness checklist version through emotional and spiritual stumbling blocks we can encounter such as, do resentments rule, am I emotionally balanced, is there something more I need to be doing, am I at peace within?

Sometimes self-care does not always mean sit quietly, close your eyes and breathe deeply. Sometimes the only path to finding your own quiet place in the sunlight is through a spiritual self-inventory, a house cleaning of sorts.

Is This the Night is an interactive workshop that offers a sampling of some wellness check exercises that can help clear the emotional clutter out to allow inner peace to find its way in. For example:

Do you keep a scorecard (some call it a hit list)?

Have you found yourself stomping into the sandbox lately?

Did you realize that control does not = Love?

Are you struggling with forgiveness?

Emerson wrote:

"What lies behind us and what lies before us are tiny matters, compared to what lies within us."

Wise man Emerson.

This workbook has been adapted by the author from the longer, retreat workshop version **to support family and friends of loved ones in a current or more recent suicidal crisis**. And we're defining "suicidal crisis" as struggling with suicidal thinking, self-injury and/or a suicide attempt. Specifically, this adaptation was created for the Zero Suicide Missouri/NAMI St. Louis *Finding Help & Hope: Supporting Loved Ones Fighting Suicide* project that is available at Mercy St. Louis and Mercy Jefferson hospitals. The exercises can still benefit those family members and friends further along their healing paths. In addition, far too many families who have already experienced a suicide loss find themselves yet again with another loved one in suicidal crisis.

Is This the Night is written as a conversation. The "voice" used reflects shared lived experiences from retreats, four years of interviewing family and friends with loved ones in suicidal crisis, as well as the author's personal commentary. As a result, the pronouns vary from "we" to "I" from time to time.

And your greatest hope moving forward is to recognize that staying connected with other family and friends of with loved ones who have also experienced a suicidal crisis is your best chance to gain some emotional balance and inner peace.

Grab a notebook, pen or pencil. Or, use your tablet or laptop. You have some note-taking and writing to do as we ease on down the road.

The Backstory

So much to say. And so much not to say! Some things are better left unsaid. But so many unsaid things can become a burden.

Virginia Mae Axline

Perfection is NOT an Asset

OK, so this may come as a bit of a shock but perfection is not an asset. It is a life-threatening liability. Dancing as fast as I could to the "society says" Dance of Perfection almost killed me, literally. I tried so hard to be perfect because then you would love me. I would be the perfect daughter, the perfect wife, the perfect mother, the perfect neighbor, the perfect employee. That didn't work out so well at any level.

Why are we having this conversation now, while you're in emotional chaos, trying to make sense of something that, in your mind, makes no sense – a suicidal crisis? Because if we don't talk about this now, things will only get worse. One of the greatest freedoms I discovered was that not only was I *not* perfect, neither was anyone else. Perfect is not attractive, likeable or anything to imitate. It sucks. Period.

Try this on for size. If I'm not perfect, and you're not perfect, then why on earth do we expect our loved ones to be perfect, get better immediately and never have another suicidal crisis?

So, before we even begin to walk through these workshop exercises and that's what this is – a series of workshops, not a "group" as in therapy, but more of a network to exchange solutions. Before we begin, let's please step back and take some deep breaths. Yes, I know. Oh, here we go with the whole breathing thing. Hate to be a spoil-sport, but breathing slowly does help calm people down.

OK, now we're ready. Well, actually, I'm ready, not sure if you are…but let's jump in anyway.

The aftermath of a catastrophic event – a tornado, a hurricane, an earthquake, tend to bring out the best in humanity. Neighborhoods and entire communities come together as never before. Complete strangers reach out to help each other through the challenging, emotional darkness.

But when the perceived catastrophe is a personal tornado, hurricane or psychological earthquake as the result of a loved one's suicide attempt or other mental health crisis, there is no outpouring of compassion and support.

You stand alone. Terrified.

And as the friends and families of suicide attempt survivors and others in suicidal crisis, you struggle to find your way free from the anxiety and stress, darkness and anger, frustration and a sense of helplessness…to find your way to the path of freedom from that fear.

Is This the Night: Finding Inner Peace is a workshop format that will gently guide participants through what some might call a spiritual and emotional inventory that will offer suggestions on how to better recognize our own behaviors and attitudes and make minor or, in some cases, major changes. This is nothing new. It's just another way to experience that turnaround to step away from fear and find inner peace. These workshops can be held weekly, twice a month or even once a month. Participation should be open and flexible.

Is This the Night: Finding Inner Peace sounds dark and serious. It is. It should. Fear can do that to people. But hope, however thin a thread, can tone it down, ease the dark to gray to a warm light – the hope that life is not meant to be *endured*, but rather to be lived fully and happily.

When fear has ruled for so long, that takes time. There's no quick fix – one brick at a time, we take down the wall that Fear built. Once in a while along the journey to freedom from fear, we may even put a brick or two back up. Eventually, if we stay focused and willing to stay on the path, if we move forward while nurturing that hope, keeping it lit like a flickering flame – unexpectedly, we will laugh out loud at something, or smile for a bit, or actually feel "OK."

This workbook is not a clinical training manual with companion PowerPoint slides and certificate of achievement. *Is This the Night: Finding Inner Peace* is a conversation, a sharing of life experience.

As one participant noted:

"*…this is what I did to fight against the fear that controlled my body, mind and soul and it really helped me to find a long lasting inner peace even in the midst of the emotional chaos and storms that may be swirling around me.*"

Another shared:

"*I had to stop obsessing over my loved one and stop, look and listen to myself. I was getting worn out. Am I taking care of myself?*"

And another:

"*I honestly didn't realize how much this crisis had changed me and not in a positive way.*"

What can we do to help support ourselves and other friends and families of suicide attempt survivors, who are emotionally drained and exhausted, worried about the loved ones – will there be yet another attempt? It's a common concern. Families of recovering alcoholics and drug addicts experience the same fear. Families of our military, active duty or returning veterans with post-traumatic stress and depression, experience the same fear. Victims of domestic abuse experience the same fear. The list is long.

It's an insidious, often unspoken fear.

The exercises outlined in this workbook may not be "the" answer, but experience has shown us that many family and friends do benefit. And as with anything, you will take away from this what you're willing to give to it.

Advocacy

Why now? (this may be a little repetitive)

The "Why Now" question – why develop *Is This the Night: Finding Inner Peace* **now** from an advocacy standpoint is answered in three parts: (1) The advocacy urged by *The Way Forward* in July 2014 as noted below; (2) the journey to find a spiritual path to recovery and healing for suicide attempt survivor families and friends. The outline for the retreat workshop was developed in late fall 2013; and (3) because there was nothing else out there for us as of September 2017. In December 2017, A Voice at the Table, a movement for Family & Friends with loved ones who have or are currently experiencing a suicidal crisis was formally launched. More about that in the Resource section.

The following is from page 35, *The Way Forward*:

http://actionallianceforsuicideprevention.org/sites/actionallianceforsuicideprevention.org/files/The-Way-Forward-Final-2014-07-01.pdf

Support for the Family and Friends of Attempt Survivors

The person recovering from a suicide attempt benefits from the support and **connectedness** that comes with having a network of people who care about them. However, the people in the network themselves often require some support and assistance.

Recommendation 2.3 – Program: Develop, evaluate, and promote programs specifically intended to help the family and friends of attempt survivors.

Supporting a person through a suicidal crisis can entail terrifying experiences and even development of secondary trauma symptoms. Yet, there are few programs that have been designed to support the family of attempt survivors, and no programs were identified for friends and other support persons. In related successful programs, trained family members (i.e., peers for family) offer groups that focus on providing education, skills, training, and support. Outcomes have included decreased stress among family members and increased coping abilities. There are also some brochures, booklets, and self-help materials designed to help family with behavioral health recovery.

The following practices might be helpful in developing efforts to assist the family and friends of attempt survivors:

● Coping strategies to avoid burnout, especially in consideration of their vigilance and help-giving efforts
● Information about the short-term and long-term factors that contribute to suicidal thinking and behavior, including those from the attempt survivor, from the family, from the environment, and from the larger culture
● Consideration of cultural and/or spiritual differences that influence support practices

Recommendation 2.4 – Practice: Expand programs and projects that provide support for families coping with mental health concerns to explicitly address issues related to suicidal crises.

There are few programs that offer support for family or friends of individuals who have been suicidal. Many people gain support from **connecting** with others while attending programs that were originally intended for educational purposes.

As a specific point for intervention, it may be helpful to have a structured meeting with family and friends when a person needs to go to a psychiatric hospital during a suicidal crisis. Resources such as groups or online forums that might foster support through connectedness for people who care about attempt survivors are desperately needed. One way to quickly foster wider availability of support is to enhance related behavioral health programs for support persons by including resources and discussion specifically about suicidal crises.

The ultimate goal is to be free, to have freedom from fear, blame, judgment, anger,
& controlling behavior –
and to find some peace within.

Some Rules about Behavior on the Emotional Roller Coaster

About those Imperfections

Author's Note: There are some pesky and annoying themes that continue to stick out and poke us as family and friends of loved ones experiencing a suicidal crisis. They fall under the didn't-we-already-have-this-conversation mode.

There is a delicate balance for a parent, spouse, partner, mentor/life coach, etc. trying to find the "right" way to do things after a suicidal crisis. Especially if we've been asked to help or, as parents of teens, required to guide those we love through the maze of life. We need to guide and support, not take hostage or smother…with the best of intentions, of course.

The more I talk with families of attempt survivors (and families of substance abusers), there is sometimes another motive behind the control: shame and discomfort that their loved one isn't perfect (ah, that word again), that they have something "wrong" with them, that they are somehow "less than" others and we screwed up. Royally.

If a person has reached a point of total despair, has lost all hope of life ever getting better – that has never been about will power or intelligence or perfection – it's about extreme, catastrophic emotional pain.

Decades ago a very wise person said to me, "Annie, start every day with this: *save me from myself and save others from me.*" And then she almost fell off the chair laughing. I wasn't impressed, but I was willing to follow her direction. It worked and still does.

And no, it was not that simple. I had to question my motives a lot. If I felt the edgy, irritable internal squirming, I had to learn to step back and actually say to myself – "Why?" What are you afraid of?" And then step back and repeat the "save others from me" mantra. I began to wrap everything with a first-do-no-harm blanket. And we can do irreparable harm verbally. It was not easy and it didn't always work, but eventually, it got easier to "let go" and not control the person or the situation. Yes! Baby steps forward.

I am a very imperfect human being. I am not super woman. I will make mistakes and that's OK. But I can also diminish the times I do by being loving and not controlling.

A suicide attempt survivor knows exactly what does *not* work. They need the freedom, respect and trust to find what does work for them. No one path is perfect. And if we disagree with choices/decisions, it's important to do so without judgement, pouting or negative attitude. That's not always easy. And if there are missteps and bumps along the way, it's not our job to fix it. Nor is it OK to continual run interference. But it is our job to be there to help when that happens, without the I-told-you-so – to just ask if there's anything we can do.

And this is really only the tip of the iceberg to developing a healthy, supportive and loving relationship with an attempt survivor as a parent, friend, spouse, or mentor. But that's an emotional challenge when we deal with depressed, self-injuring and suicidal teens or adults. We want them fixed and now! We want them to "happy" and well and OK! And we will go to hell and back to make that happen. The problem is that "we" cannot always make anything happen.

There's a fine line between assertive advocacy and flat out control. And it's very hard to support loved ones and not worry or allow fear to drive us. These are our kids, parents, siblings, best friends. We know from scientific data that our loved ones feel a sense of burden that they are disrupting our lives. We need to be careful to respond to the crisis, not react out of fear.

We are all imperfect beings. But if we will make time to sit and really listen to our loved ones without judgement and with compassion, together we can walk through this crisis minute by minute, hour by hour, day by day.

Exercise: Your workshop facilitator will launch a round-robin discussion around the table. If you are at home, alone, just write down random thoughts about what you just read,

The Bear Hugs Kettle Snag

I have way too many meditation books scattered around the house. *Around the Year with Emmet Fox* is not my all-time favorite, but his February 23rd "Bear Hugs Kettle" meditation is. Getting tangled in the "Bear Hugs Kettle" web can negatively impact my entire life – and it took time to recognize that and make the needed changes.

Allow me to paraphrase:

Out in the West, a group of hunters had their day's catch cooking in a huge kettle over the camp fire. Something distracted them and they left the campsite for a bit. An old bear comes out of the woods and walks into the camp drawn by the aroma of the kettle's contents.

As bears will do, he grabbed the kettle. It burned him. But rather than let go, he pulled it closer and closer to crush it. The more he did, the more it burned, so he hugged it tighter, and it burned him even more until he died. To live, the bear needed to let go.

Fox's spiritual lesson was that so many of us tend to hold onto our "comfort zones" even when they may be hurting us, holding us back from happiness, even killing us. He suggests that when we find ourselves doing that, to think, "bear hugs kettle," and let go completely.

I held on to an abusive marriage because it was my "comfort zone." It almost killed me.

Fear can generate thoughts and behaviors that become our "comfort zones."

"Bear hugs kettle." Let go.

Exercise: Let's give some thought to whether or not we may have a few bear-hugs-kettle-snags within our lives today. And please keep in mind, our focus is on our actions and attitudes, not those of our loved ones.

How Did It Come to This?

Where is the horse and the rider? Where is the horn that was blowing? They have passed like rain on the mountain, like wind in the meadow. The days have gone down in the West behind the hills into shadow. How did it come to this?

King Theoden, Lord of the Rings: The Two Towers

In a scene in the *Lord of the Rings* trilogy, faced with a devastating crisis, the king wonders, "How did it come to this?" He didn't look to blame anyone. In bewilderment, he just posed the question out loud, and determined to help his people, led them into battle.

If you're not familiar with the story line, by themselves, they would not have succeeded, but help came in time to wrap around the "enemy" and together, the battle was won. It is a story of resilience, hope and connections.

Family members and close friends of loved ones who have had a recent suicidal crisis often find themselves in the same position: how did it come to this? When we are faced with a world-shattering, personal crisis such as a suicide attempt, it's human and instinctive to want to lash out and blame someone or something. The fear and confusion is no less when we are trying to understand and support a loved one who self-injures or struggles with suicidal thinking.

The answers to the "how did it come to this" may eventually be answered. But right now, the focus needs to be on what do we – not "I" – what do we as family/friends do next? Your loved one will have a plan of action, a safety framework, counseling, maybe in-patient care and more. Those will be the first steps of a long journey, and as family and friends, we want to support them in every way we can.

Before beginning this workbook and the sessions ahead, let's consider what those who have come before us in this situation learned – those who know exactly how we feel – as they began their journey to healing and inner peace.

- Eliminate the word blame from your vocabulary and your thoughts.
- Do not blame anyone, including yourself.
- Stop searching and prodding for "reasons why." They will be revealed over time.
- Recognize that you need to do something about *your* inner fears and anger.

- Accept that this workshop series is not something to put off and do "later." The content needs to be addressed now if you truly want to help and support your loved one.
- None of this will be easy but, in the long run, incredibly beneficial all around.

Exercise: Let's take time to discuss these bullets. We will come back and review this page in a few weeks.

What? Me Color?

Materials required:

Coloring books from Stuff2Color.com or similar resource, Sharpies, Doodle Pads

There is research available to support the use of coloring for adults. Most participants who come to the table may be reluctant to even try, but we have found that if the facilitator is gently persuasive, the majority will give it a try. For those who won't, it's important to have some form of Doodle Pad available for them to use.

For families and friends further along the healing path, we introduce the coloring/doodle materials out of the gate. For those who are still fresh off a crisis, waiting a session or two may work better, but have the materials available from Day One, just in case.

The healing conversation for this Me Color? exercise centers around:

What helps distract you or helps you to unwind and are you utilizing that consistently to maintain an emotional balance?

"I have to admit, I thought this was silly...until I gave it a try and realized that it actually helped calm my anxiety and help me to better focus on the discussion around the table."

- Father of a teen suicide attempt survivor

Frozen in Time

In one week, I received texts or direct messages in the middle of the night from four different families. Their loved ones were in various emergency departments for some form of suicidal crisis. Each one said the exact same thing: I didn't think it would be my kid.

Annemarie Matulis

As family and friends of those in a suicidal crisis, disbelief that it's "our" loved one in danger is common. So are some of the questions that race across our minds like a ticker-tape:

- I was planning a trip next month. Should I cancel it?
- I should withdraw from my volunteer work so I'm around more, right?
- Should I ask for family leave from my job?
- Should I resign from my job to stay home?
- (for adults) Do I need to get someone to stay with them all the time?
- (for adolescents and teens) Do I let them go back to school, stay in their clubs or on their sports teams, etc.?

In other words, do we as the family and friends with loved ones in suicidal crisis remain frozen in time?

The answer is as individual as each of us. This in not black or white and one size does not fit all. Short term, some of those actions may be needed. Staying frozen in time long term will prove a disaster for everyone. This was the concern expressed in the National Action Alliance's *The Way Forward* (2014): the potential burn out that can impact caregivers (us) of those in suicidal crisis.

Let's try this exercise to uncover what our "frozen in time" questions might be:

- Take about 10 to 15 minutes and write them down.
- No editing.
- No trying to sound "nice," or emotionally balanced, or all together with no concerns.
- The "I've-got-this" denial syndrome doesn't work either.

One key to inner peace in this area is to uncover the lived experiences of those who stumbled along this path before you. Another is to be totally open and honest within the workshop setting and support each other to find answers that fit. But again, what works for one family may not be a good fit for another. Be OK with that and support each other.

And be very aware that the underlying fear in some of our choices is driven by the nagging thought, "…will this happen again?" That's a much longer conversation for another time – and sooner rather than later, but the short answer? Quite possibly.

Is it OK to be Angry?

Oxford defines anger as: *A strong feeling of annoyance, displeasure, or hostility*

The American Psychological Association defines anger as: *an emotion characterized by antagonism toward someone or something you feel has deliberately done you wrong. **Anger** can be a good thing. It can give you a way to express negative feelings, for example, or motivate you to find solutions to problems.*

There are some that suggest that anger is really fear-driven emotion and behavior.

How do *you* define anger? The question is rhetorical, but take a few minutes and give it some thought. Feel free to jot your thoughts down on paper.

There is a bit of twist when it comes to a suicidal crisis. Many family and friends are reluctant to say out loud that they are angry with their loved ones. After all, that pesky "society says" dance says that we shouldn't be angry with someone who is not well. It goes a little like this:

- Am I a bad parent if I'm angry about this situation?
- What would people say if I admit I am angry?
- What do I do with these feelings?
- What else have you been thinking that fits in here?

Confused? Welcome to the world of family and friends of those who experience a suicidal crisis. In this workshop, or even sitting at home, this is the time to openly, honestly and safely, let loose with those emotions and thoughts so you can embrace them, acknowledge them and then use them to guide you to seek out solutions for yourself – not your loved one, not yet.

We are not bad people to feel angry. However, if we don't get this outside of ourselves, if we don't admit and accept this, the internal chaos can become a nightmare, long term.

Let's do this. Let's begin this conversation.

Exercise:

In a group setting? Your facilitator will guide the activities.

On your own at home with this? Begin with journaling. No editing. Just raw writing. But it's important that you have someone you trust implicitly with whom to share this (a counselor, best friend, etc.). This is not a solitary journey. We have found over the years that it is the connection with others who are on the same path that helps enhance and expedite the healing. If you happen to be in some form of 12-Step modality, your sponsor is the obvious choice.

In addition, we are establishing a closed group on Facebook so participants can exchange progress, lessons learned and other information with each other and continue the conversation. It is a safe haven, but it is not a crisis response setting.

For information contact: director@avoiceatthetable.org

Taking a Walk Might Save *My* Life?

The first thing we hear at the retreat workshop is a rapid response as to why walking is not an option. As the facilitator, I allow about 3 minutes of that noise and then say, *"Really? If your life depended on this? That's pure B.S."* While that does tend to offend a few – OK, it offends everyone, it does quiet everyone down. The usual suspects for the not working include things like:

I don't have time to do that.

I don't have anywhere to walk.

I have bad knees (feet, shoulders, hands, fingers)

And the one I love best: *"I'm not the one with mental health concerns or in suicidal crisis."*

Wow! Holy Al-Anon newcomer! (**Author's note**: years ago, family members with an active or even recovering alcoholic were guided to Al-Anon. Their push back was, "Why? I'm not the one who was drinking").

OK. Why don't we step back a moment and begin again?

If you are the family or friend of a loved one who recently attempted suicide or had another form of suicidal crisis, please – *please* give some serious thought to some form of physical activity for yourself and connecting with that outdoor/Nature thing.

We all have more time in our day than we recognize. If you were asked to find 15 minutes within your day, the process would be to break out everything you do in 15-minute increments for two or three days. And that means **Everything**.

Example. Several years ago, I stopped, looked around and realized that I was standing in the living room, shoes and coat still on. I had just spent the last 20 minutes surfing the guide to 300 plus channels, including the Spanish, French, Portuguese and Russian ones (I speak only English – but I did study Latin and French for 6 years!). What hit me up the side of the head was that I did that every day of the week, sometimes twice a day. That adds up to about 4 ½ hours a week.

If we, as family and friends, are brutally honest, we can all find a little bit of time.

Exercise:
Next is the "nowhere to walk" brick wall. Let's give this some thought and exchange ideas with each other.

- Your neighborhood
- The mall
- A park nearby
- Riverfront
- A local gym with treadmills

Now, those are the obvious but they all do have concerns for some. The most immediate is access, time of day, etc. At the retreat, this about the spot that I share that I am a person with a visual impairment, the result of three untreated skull fractures in that abusive marriage. That does tend to quiet the room down again. I have not been behind the wheel of a car in more than 34 years. So, getting out to any of the potential sites listed above is not an option for me.

I walk every day. The ultimate goal is 10,000 steps a day, just because. Actually, I once read that the actor Jeff Goldblum walked 10,000 steps a day and thought that sounded like a good number. I'm currently at 7,500.

How do I do that? Much of the steps are the result of my daily activity but a percent – that fits into that "15 minute" category gets done in the house. Yup. I walk around in the house with no goal except to clear my head. That can be done in one or two rooms, or in a cavern like the 270-year old colonial I live in, alleged resident ghost and all.

And someone always pushes back and says something like "that's ridiculous" or "I can't do that, there's no room."

No one has ever been able to more clearly define "ridiculous" and I usually demonstrate how easy it is to move around, walk back and forth, rock back and forth to music or during commercials, in a small space **if you are motivated.**

It helps with stress, anxiety, depression…and most people end up smiling, if only a little bit. It may be more than they have smiled in while. Try it. Please.

Exercise: When you return to the next session, plan to share what you did with this.

Walked 15 minutes a day

Joined a gym

Walked around the house (waving arms or singing loudly is optional)

Moved from the couch to chair (just kidding – what? You did?)

Signed up for a marathon

"Other" (what the hell does that mean anyway?)

The Sandbox

Yup! The SANDBOX! Nice visual, huh? Maybe not...

So, let's talk about the sandbox, shall we? Allow me to share a story.

Picture a well-dressed woman in very high heels stepping into a sandbox. She seems upset, perhaps angry or frustrated because she can't seem to get her point across to someone. The more powerfully she argues her point, the deeper her high heels sink into the sand.

Better yet, perhaps the debate is about who is right and who is wrong. And our well-dressed woman (or man) sinks deeper and deeper into the sand as they verbally beat the other person seeking to achieve victory and total surrender via an admission that they are R-I-G-H-T!

Well, I was told a long time ago by a very wise woman that this is a case of being so right, that I'm dead wrong. And then she asked me how it felt to wrap that visual around myself – at my age (then 37), heels dug into the sand, kicking it around, just to win an argument or make sure someone knew that I *was* right?

Not a very attractive visual.

But fear can make us do silly things. As a battered woman, I had become terrorized by another person and was never allowed the opportunity to have my point of view heard. So in the beginning of my healing journey, I fought to have my voice heard. I fought harder when I worried that someone I cared about – a friend, a co-worker, someone I was mentoring, might be at risk for harm – making bad choices, engaging in risky or self-destructive behaviors – driven by F-E-A-R.

Fear can manifest itself in controlling behavior. Controlling behavior in any relationship/friendship is lethal. Love and Control are not friends.

As family and friends of loved ones in a recent suicidal crisis, we tend to jump into the Sandbox with both feet. And that communication problem can crop up over the years if fear gets triggered again. And it can and it does.

So the Wellness Check Question is: What is my current relationship with the Sandbox?

Exercise: Take out your notebook and spend at least 20 minutes writing down whatever comes to mind about this topic. If you approach it honestly, the words will come.

If you are working within a group, the facilitator will guide you all through a discussion of what you discovered about your current behaviors and the Sandbox. Always keep in mind that the only behavior we are investigating is our own, not that of our loved ones.

When you're done writing and discussing, turn the page – literally, and jot down 3 things that make you smile instantly

Now go do something fun, light and easy.

Forgiveness – the most difficult part of the journey

The greatest gift I was given and my first step to healing was the ability to laugh…and most importantly, to laugh at myself – not ridicule, not demean – but to see the humor in my thinking and behavior while allowing myself to say inwardly, "And they think I'm so perfectly altogether."

It took a long time to forgive – to forgive the abuser, to forgive my family, to forgive God, but the hardest of all, was to forgive myself for not being P-E-R-F-E-C-T.

Annemarie Matulis, *Is This the Night Retreat Workshop*

In any crisis situation, we need to be able to step back and let go of the negative self-talk. In a suicidal crisis, even more so.

What did I miss?

Why didn't I see this coming?

Why didn't I listen better?

Am I a bad parent? Friend?

Why am I angry at them? That's wrong, right?

So now is the time to grab a notebook, some loose paper or whatever you're comfortable using to begin writing to adapt these examples to you.

Is This the Night: Finding Inner Peace is intended to be a suicide prevention protective factor. Families and friends of suicide attempt survivors can be at increased risk. This is about life and death. Tip toeing around this topic is not an option.

In a safeTALK suicide prevention gatekeeper training, we stress the importance to not, "Miss, Dismiss or Avoid" the invitations presented by those with suicidal thoughts. In this case, we need to be careful to not miss, dismiss or avoid the need to forgive – ourselves, first and foremost.

Now, about those examples of who and what might be on your "Forgiveness List":

- YOU
- Your suicide attempt survivor (or other loved one)

If your process is not specific to a suicide attempt survivor, just adjust the list of who and what to meet your needs.

- Clinicians – for not "fixing" your attempt survivor
- Doctors – same as above
- Hospitals – same as above
- E.R personnel – same as above
- Other family members/friends – for dismissing the importance of the issue; lack of support (it's important to list people out individually, not lump them all together).
- God – or whatever you believe in; if you don't have a spiritual reference, try "the universe, Karma, fate…or put it back to YOU.

As you continue in this journey to freedom and inner peace, you may stumble across a few more to add to the list. Don't hesitate to do that.

How to begin? Anger and resentment might work (said with a smile).

Ask yourself some basic questions and then write about it in your notebook. For example, we'll assume you love your attempt survivor (loved one for others) but just wish they could be "well," and not be at risk any more.

Can you acknowledge how you really feel about that?

Do you sometimes get frustrated, angry, and/or resentful about the time and energy taken away from you, your own family, job, vacation, personal dreams, etc.?

It's perfectly normal to have those negative feelings and more. We are imperfect human beings, something we can often lose sight of in a crisis and stressful situation.

However, the "society says" dance can create a chaotic battleground within.

Negative self-talk can be deadly:

- *What an awful person I am to be angry and resentful with someone who has a serious public health issue.*

- *Would I think that way if it was cancer or heart failure?*

- *He/she is family. I should do better.*

Really?

Many, many wise women and men have shared over the centuries the same statement about forgiveness. It's never about forgetting the fear – it's about ***not*** allowing that part of our lives to control, dictate or hold me emotional hostage ever again; to be free in the truest sense.

And let's be really clear, we are not seeking to forgive the attempt survivor in our life for the suicide attempt(s) – (or those from other situations, e.g., substance abuse, PTSD, etc.). That is *not* forgiveness in any sense; that is bone crushing, self-pity dripping, self-righteous superiority as ugly as it gets.

We are forgiving *how* that behavior terrified us. And that kind of fear will manifest in so many ways, so very often as anger – but no matter how you dress it up, it's F-E-A-R. And if we can't let go of that fear or frankly won't let go of it, the internal war with stress and anxiety will rule. And it's an emotional and psychological war that will bring countless battles.

So, let's step back at this point and do some writing and or sharing:

Go back to the "Forgiveness List". Is it complete or do you have more to add?

Can you *now* acknowledge how you really feel about that?

Do you sometimes get frustrated, angry, and/or resentful about the time and energy taken away from you, your own family, job, vacation, personal dreams, etc.?

This has probably been a very emotional conversation. Let's stop for now and end with this:

Share one thing that instantly brings a smile to your face.

Fear plus Control does *not* = Love.

We mean well. We're human, after all. We want to do everything we can to support and protect our loved ones. We want them to be safe.

Sadly, that typically translates into fear driven control. We are the last to see that and unfortunately, we may not "see" it until it's too late and we have done irreparable harm to the very ones we were trying to support.

So, how do we recognize our own destructive behavior and when we do, how can we change it?

First, it takes a willingness to admit we need to amend our behavior, then we have to become extremely open to information that can help and then, toughest of all, we need to adopt a life or death commitment to change. Sound radical? Not really. Not if our fear driven control is pushing our loved one away from us, perhaps forever.

We mean well, we do, and we can do good, we can, but – big BUT – if we admit and accept that perhaps we have been hostage to fear driven control, we must change *ourselves*, not our loved one and then we really can do good.

So, where to begin?

Self-evaluation Exercise:

Have I been rationalizing that my behavior is loving, when if I'm honest, I've really been trying to control their every move (under the guise of helping them stay safe)?

What am I afraid will happen if I "let go" of this control (they might attempt suicide again, they might go back to drugs or alcohol, etc.)?

Have I been so controlling/dominating that my loved one is totally dependent upon me? If I "let go," am I afraid they will leave?

Love is not control.

So let's add another wrinkle into the conversation: why do you get angry? Why do you get angry, upset, annoyed when your loved wants to do something new, or different, or without you? Or actually does do any or all of that but didn't ask "permission"?

Trying to control another person is a set up for nightmare of emotional and verbal battles, one after the other. That takes a terrible toll on everyone. And that is not love.

So, let's talk about this – together.

The Sandbox – Part II

Seriously? You didn't think it was that easy, did you?

OK, new variation of the sandbox.

I'm not sure how many of you are familiar with Lois Wilson? Her husband, Bill, was one of the co-founders of Alcoholics Anonymous, the grandfather of the 12 Step modality from which many self-help programs evolved.

Lois dedicated her life to trying to "fix" Bill's serious drinking problem. She tried everything. If you don't know the story, Bill eventually did stop drinking. He got sober. But not because of Lois, but rather due to the work he did with other alcoholics seeking to recover. Today, we call this kind of work in the mental health arena and many other areas Peer to Peer – and most states have a training protocol to actually certify the profession.

There came a point when Lois recognized that she was pretty ticked off that a handful of sober drunks helped her husband find the spiritual breakthrough he needed to stop drinking. And she jumped into the sandbox. And from that anger and resentment, the world was blessed with Al-Anon Family Groups. Al-Anon members encourage their loved ones to do whatever it takes to get sober and remain "happy, joyous and free."

And there are two outcomes from this sandbox story:

(1) That perhaps one of the most powerful group of people who can be of support and help to our attempt survivor are other healing , healthy and happy attempt survivors. And we should let that happen.

(2) That similar to the family and friends of alcoholics actively self-harming (drinking) or sober, we (friends/family of suicide attempt survivors) also need to work daily on our own inventory – our own wellness checks, our own emotional and spiritual wellbeing.

…and do our best to stay out of the sandbox, or allow fear to dictate our thinking and behavior, or try to control our loved ones into wellness and safety…

It's not our job to "fix" anyone but ourselves.

Love does not = fixing someone unless that someone = me.

Exercise: Wellness Check/Inventory Question: How well are you doing or did you do to encourage your attempt survivor to seek support (not *your* I'll-FIX-it way, but theirs)?

Step away from the notebook – stretch, walk around the room, step outside and look at the sky…

You are now one step closer to emotional freedom.

Attitudes & Actions – Mine, Not Yours

This exercise will be overlap other work each session.

In the middle of difficulty lies opportunity.

Albert Einstein

While filming one of our "Voices" series documentaries, *Voices from the Shadows*, Paula, a loss survivor and the mother of a suicide attempt survivor, was in conversation with three other parents of attempt survivors. Sitting with them was Tracey Pacheco Medeiros, a suicide attempt survivor – "my" suicide attempt survivor.

Tracey is almost 20 years into her healing path from her last attempt. When Paula asked Tracey what helped her make the turnaround to life, the reply was that one of the most important components was behavior modification. There a number of variations, but Tracey was enrolled for two years in a DBT (Dialectical Behavior Therapy) class.

Paula acknowledged that in trying to better understand how to support her son, she had thrown herself into DBT also. From behind the camera, I said, "Me too." Please do not mistake this as a blanket endorsement of DBT. Keep in mind that in other exercises we have stressed that there is no one-size-fits-all for anyone. But family and friends of loved ones in recent suicidal crisis, may want to take a peek. As Einstein suggests, this may be a life-changing opportunity within a very difficult situation.

What Paula and I both discovered was, that with the best of intentions, and perhaps a tad too much education (yes, I really said that), we were saying and doing all the wrong things to our loved ones. We had to relearn how to communicate, how much language matters, tone of voice matters, that day to day, the emotional roller coaster can be incredibly frustrating. But we also found that implementing the tools from DBT did make a positive difference for us personally as well as with our ability to better communicate with our loved ones.

But I do not want to mislead you, communication with your loved one may continue to be problematic from time to time.

Note: This will be one of the more difficult challenges and requires brutal honesty. And while it's not "too soon" to dig this deep into **you**r personal inventory related to **your** attitudes and actions that impact your loved one and others around you, we strongly suggest that this is only discussed in general terms within the group using the prompts below. When you decide that is time to begin this process, you will work on it for several weeks or more. We also recommend that you not do this particular exercise without support – a friend, mentor, counselor, sponsor, etc.

Guidance: The best way to complete this exercise is to set aside 15 minutes a couple of times a week to address the prompts. As with any emotional process, it's always important and helpful to balance the hard work with something more fun and relaxing as well as some fresh air and walking.

Discussion prompts within a group:

Question 1: Is it possible that, with the best on intentions, you may need to consider some behavior modification of your own?

Reflect back on the exercises like the Sandbox, Anger, Bear Hugs Kettle, Control Does Not = Love, and Forgiveness, etc.

Check point example: if your interactions with your loved one are always in "battle" mode, the answer to question 1 might well be, "Yes."

Question 2: Can you remain calm and focused when discussing the recent suicidal crisis with your loved one? If not, how can you adjust that attitude?

Question 3: Have you made progress with controlling issues? Explain.

Question 4: Have you sat down with and listened to your loved one to uncover what phrases and behaviors of yours are upsetting to them? Are you able to make the coping skills changes?

Question 5: Have you participated in suicide prevention trainings to help ease your own stress and anxiety about being more aware of invitations?

What trainings?

What was your take-away?

What more do you feel you need to know to help you maintain your emotional balance?

There are countless tools available to help expand this process. And please don't allow yourself to push these away because the original targeted population is not a fit for you. They are tools that contain spiritual principles that can be very helpful to us – family and friends of loved ones in suicidal crisis, in part because there just isn't much of anything out there specific to us (we are working on it):

- As of December 2017, www.avoiceatthetable.org is developing into a national "safe haven" of information and resources.
- There is also an informational Facebook page: https://www.facebook.com/Is-This-the-Night-125437314912158/
- If you happen to be in a 12th Step recovery program, this would fall under a 10th Step Checklist process (assuming you have done work on your 4th Step inventory).
- If not, you can purchase a copy of Al-Anon's *Blueprint for Progress, Al-Anon's Fourth Step Inventory* from Hazeldon or Al-Anon's web site, or check your local library, and substitute the word "alcohol" with "suicidal."
- If you happen to have a copy of Julia Cameron's *The Artist's Way* laying around, dust it off and begin the process again (and don't get caught up in the avoidance of "I'm not an artist – this exercise applies to anyone).
- A copy of *Co-Dependent No More* or the companion meditation workbook, *The Language of Letting Go*

Who Am I?

There was I time before my arthritis got to be a real pain that I could actually get on my knees. And throughout my healing and recovery from the violence, I found comfort to pray on my knees. It's not for everyone and I no longer do that. I mean, I do begin and end every day in prayer and meditation – yeah, I really do that. I just don't do it on my knees.

*Anyway, that wasn't the point! I was a bit tired this particular morning, complaining about it must be an age thing (I was 50), which is pretty laughable now 21 years later...**anyway!** I was being quiet, an empty head, no ticker-tape running, and heard the question, "What is the meaning of my life?" Like, what the hell? Who said that?*

What was more unsettling than the question and who said it was that I had no answer. None. Nada. Total silence. I can tell you that's not a very comfortable space to be in. And then, the answer slowly formed in my head: to be of service to others. And I thought I had a handle on that...until two years later, we almost lost Tracey in her last suicide attempt.

Annemarie Matulis, *Is This the Night: Finding Inner Peace* Retreat Workshop

As family and friends of a loved one who has recently experienced a suicidal crisis, we may find ourselves struggling to answer the "Who am I?" and "What happens now?" questions. If you have participated in this workshop series over the last few weeks/months, you may not have an easy answer to those questions. Ideally, you've learned a lot about yourself, your attitudes, behaviors, self-awareness, your relationships with loved ones, and your need to prioritize your self-care. And perhaps you've made some adjustments and changes based on what you've discovered. So, let's talk about that, OK?

Exercise:

Let's crack out the notebooks again and do some writing, jot a few thoughts down.

How do you identify/describe yourself? Is it any different than when you stepped into this workshop series? Have you identified attitudes and behaviors that you agree need some work? Explain what you've done to achieve that.

Discrimination & Prejudice = Stigma

When a loved one breaks a leg or is in some kind of accident, everyone jumps in and asks how they can help. When you announce that you're raising funds for someone with cancer, the world applauds. No one ever says: Hey, how's your suicide attempt survivor doing?"

*Welcome to my world. Welcome to the world of millions – **millions** of parents, family and friends of those across the lifespan, young and older, who self-injure, struggle constantly with thoughts of suicide and/or attempt suicide.*

Voices from the Shadows documentary

There are so many threads to this discussion: prejudice, discrimination, irrational guilt and shame, concerns about judgement from others, isolation – it can be a very lonely, frightening and confusing place emotionally and mentally. And at the moment (2017), there is not much structured or clinical guidance available to help you walk through the maze. We have decades of research gathered about suicide grief support for loss survivors. More recently, supports for suicide attempt survivors have emerged, but not in great numbers.

What we do have is the lived experience from people like me and other family and friends of loved ones in a suicidal crisis. What follows are some snippets to share how we began those early steps to our own wellness.

To begin this session, ask each person to read one of the quotes. Discussion will follow after they have all been read.

(1) First and foremost, break the silence. Your loved one has a public health issue, they are not criminals. You are not a bad parent or friend and your loved one is not "damaged" or less of a person than if they were battling cancer or diabetes. It's the secrecy and silence that perpetuates the prejudice.

(2) My instinct was to learn everything I could about depression, self-injury and suicide. Then I realized I was focusing on my loved one, not on how to take better care of myself so I could help them. Major revelation!

(3) People don't know what to say, so they say stupid things or avoid talking to me.

(4) I decided to just talk, talk, talk to everyone about having a family member who struggled with suicidal thinking. I was stunned at how many people said, "Yeah. Me, too." But many had never said that out loud or talked to anyone else about it.

(5) I spent hours on the Internet trying to find information that would help me not feel like I was going to melt down myself. Nothing. Nothing! And then I was at a training and heard the instructor identify herself as the "family of one, and friend of many suicide attempt survivors." I did a "thumbs up" to go to the rest room…and cried. I wasn't alone.

(6) People were f#%@&$! Ignorant. So I educated them and began to realize how much better I felt.

(7) I sat the whole family down and told them about my own experiences with depression and a suicide attempt in my 20's. They were stunned. Then angry that I had never shared this before, but within in minutes, hugged me, and we all cried. Her comment was "you really do understand." As a parent, I wish I had shared that sooner.

Exercise:

Sadly, a suicidal crisis which is a public health issue can often shatter a family's beliefs, sense of balance and wellness, and leave everyone struggling to find even ground again. Education is a powerful tool.

Consider the following points for discussion and share potential solutions:

- prejudice
- discrimination
- irrational guilt and shame
- concerns about judgement from others
- isolation

Before you go…never, never forget that while you may feel powerless and angry and frightened right now, you do have power over your attitude and actions. Be kind to everyone around you and most importantly, be kind to yourself.

Birds sing after a storm, why shouldn't people feel as free to delight in whatever remains to them?

Rose Fitzgerald Kennedy

First item on your gratitude list – your loved one might be in crisis, but they are alive. Reason for celebration…make sure you share that with them, too.

And when you've done that, then go out and kick-ass educate the ignorant. You'll feel great!

Reflections

The exercises that you just completed were specifically developed for a workshop process for those with a loved one who has had a more recent suicidal crisis but they can be applied to anyone at any point along the healing path.

As noted earlier, the original workbook and retreat workshop were designed for the families who have journeyed much further along the healing path. The pages that follow are snippets of what we use in that retreat workshop. A little bit of history and backstory (you may find some of the information familiar from the work you've already done).

If you feel you've made some progress, give them a try. No. Seriously. Try them. You have nothing to lose and a lot more to gain. A word of caution, if you have not completed all of the previous exercises, the next few may be a tad more difficult.

Journaling – the Forever Journey

"Never happen." – that's what I so often hear when I suggest that the friends and family of suicide attempt survivors sit down and begin to use this important spiritual tool.

"I can't write."

"I don't have time."

"I don't know what to say."

"Isn't that a therapy thing?"

And a thousand more barriers get thrown up to prevent them from at least trying it.

So when I share that journaling probably helped save my life as I took those first baby steps free from abuse and fear, the opponents quiet down a bit. If you search Amazon Books (assuming it still exists when you read this) for "journal writing," about 2,000 options come up. We know that human-kind have been writing down their thoughts and experiences in one way or another for centuries.

I'm not about to offer a scientific dissertation as to why journaling can help a person keep in an emotional and spiritual balance. What I can share is that I've been using it as an inner peace tool since 1983 – daily, without exception I write something and that has helped me keep a healthy perspective on **my** behavior (not anyone else's). And that perspective helps me keep on track.

It's that simple. There's no right or wrong about it, there's no "one way only" to do it. Friends and family of suicide attempt survivors need an outlet to express themselves safely. Journaling can do that. In *the Artist's Way*, author Julie Cameron urges participants to set aside a brief time to do the "Morning Pages," a three page exercise of putting unedited, random thoughts down on paper. In today's age, I suppose many might use their tablets, laptops, PC's and even their phones to do this. I still prefer to put pen to paper which doesn't come easy with arthritis.

The goal?

Simple – to help clear our heads, hearts and souls of the noise swirling around internally.

Exercise:

Grab 3 sheets of paper, or a notebook, whatever works for you.

Take a deep breath and exhale (yup, that breathing thing again).

For the next 15 minutes just write whatever comes to mind.

If you find yourself stuck – write, "I'm stuck and don't know what to write because I don't do this on a daily basis…" and see what follows.

You do not need to make sense

Do not worry about grammar, spelling or sentence structure – this is not an essay.

Do NOT edit!

So, now let's talk about this for a bit…

If you are not at a retreat with us, settle in for a moment to take a self-observation. Or, if you have registered for the closed Facebook page, you can engage with others there.

The Score Card

Anger is meant to be listened to. Anger is a voice, a shout, a plea a demand.

Anger is meant to be acted upon.

Anger is not meant to acted out.

With a little thought, we can usually translate the message that our anger is sending us.

~ Julia Cameron, "Recovering a Sense of Power," *The Artist's Way*

Hopefully, if you are participating in this workshop, you have let go of two of the R's of Anger – revenge and retaliation. Sadly, the deadliest of the three is resentment – the ***Score Card***. The 3 R's of Anger are typically the direct result of someone not doing what we want them to do, the way we want them to do it, when we want them to do it. Annoying, right?

Example: someone driving recklessly can threaten our safety. He/she is not driving the way we want them to and as a result, we may feel threatened. And we get angry. And shout things and make impolite gestures…and then we tell at least 100 people about, or better yet, go on social media and tell the world. And we continue to fan the flames of that fear and anger. That's a textbook resentment. Some define it as "reliving a situation over and over." Nothing good ever comes from that.

And let's more clearly define the "Score Card." The person who forgot your birthday, or the one who didn't call you back, or the one who didn't bring a gift…actually, I have a friend who calls it his "hit list."

The good news is that many people honestly don't get buried under resentments or the **Score Card.** But some do and it can create a very negative emotional life. And as difficult as it is to admit, we can often slide our loved one onto that list

This can happen if we have not paid attention to our own spiritual wellness. We can easily slip back into "poor me" mode of:

All that I gave up for you.

All the times I sat home worrying if you were OK.

All the times you didn't call and let me know that you were home safe.

And the list can go on. And that's an unhealthy and unacceptable state of mind not to mention deadly to any friendship or family relationship.

Exercise: **So, taking a quick Wellness Self-Inventory check – how are you doing these days with resentments? Do you still have a Score Card?**

Let's do some writing. And then let's do some talking.

Grace and Meditation

I'm not clear on how or why Grace happens. There are people far more qualified to explain that. Most of us know the lyrics of "Amazing Grace" but many just sing the song and don't stop to consider the meaning.

Nor am I at all religious. I do adhere to a spiritual life path and I do have experiences in my life that I can only attribute to what I refer to as "God's Amazing Grace." You don't have to embrace that but I do believe it happens. I call them "God tangibles" – that light that suddenly shines in the dark so you can see where you're walking…

By all medical explanation, I should be dead, and I'm not. X-rays and scans reveal that there are any number of fractures in my head that should have killed me on the spot. I cannot even begin to count the number of concussions I experienced over a fifteen year period. Something I do worry about today with all the talk about CTE (Chronic Traumatic Encephalopathy).

I also believe we haven't even touched the tip of the iceberg about the human ability to heal, but that's a conversation for another time.

For me, grace and meditation go hand in hand. Ironically, meditation is one skill I cannot teach others well. I meditate every morning and every evening – no exceptions. It's a key to my inner peace. I can even shut down within a crowd for a few seconds to recapture that state of mind. But, to me, meditation is so personal, I just have not found a good way to teach it.

What has worked for many, many people I've mentored is using a meditation book every day. Which one you use does not matter. Just be consistent. I often suggest reading the day's "message" three or four times in a row. To me, that is a form of meditation.

One of the primary aspects of meditation is completely clearing my mind of any thoughts, to just allow my brain to empty and be present to receive inner peace and calm.

Exercise:

If you do meditate, explain how you achieve that state of mind and how long have you been using this spiritual tool? Remember, we're having a conversation, this is not a training. Talk to me on paper.

If you don't meditate, share with me why not? Do you think you might consider trying it? Or at least picking up a meditation book and give yourself a month of reading the daily messages?

Talk to me on paper.

And then we'll share it with the workshop.

More Backstory

Why?

(From 2015)

There's a lot of emphasis on "why" as we open this retreat workshop. Why the title – *Is This the Night?* It sounds dark and serious. It is. It does. It should. Fear can do that to people. But hope, however thin a thread, can tone it down, ease the dark to gray to a warm light – the hope that life is not meant to be *endured*, but rather to be lived fully and happily.

When fear has ruled for so long, that takes time. There's no quick fix – one brick at a time, we take down the wall that fear built. Once in a while along the journey to freedom from fear, we may even put a brick or two back up. Eventually, if we stay focused and willing to stay on the path, if we move forward while nurturing that hope, keeping it lit like a flickering flame – unexpectedly, we will laugh out loud at something, or smile for a bit, or actually feel "OK."

And while the workbook can be useful to a number of groups, why the emphasis on the friends and families of suicide attempt survivors? Why that group and why now? The answer is simple: there is a need. Just as there was a need 30-35 years ago to bang the drum for domestic violence, to write about it, to change laws, to create shelters, to change the clinical approach to victims and to educate law enforcement, the military and so many others about how to deal with all aspects of domestic violence. And yet prejudice and discrimination still worm their way into the public discussion about violence related to families and relationships.

We've spent decades and billions on fighting alcoholism and drug addiction. And we're still not sure how well that worked out for this country.

And then there's suicide. We are blessed to have resources for loss survivors – those left behind by the death of a loved. We need much more. We are grateful that doors are being cracked open to recognize the value of the lived and learned experience and expertise of suicide attempt survivors. With that said, as you read this, there is next to nothing to help support friends and families of suicide attempt survivors to find their way free from the anxiety and stress, darkness and anger, frustration and a sense of helplessness…to find their way to the path of freedom from fear.

Is This the Night is not "the" answer but, hopefully, it will not only help those in need to that path, but gently nudge them a bit as they ease on down the road and eventually find their own place in the bright sunlight of hope. And just about anyone and everyone can benefit from a bit of a wellness check now and again.

This retreat workshop is not a clinical training with companion PowerPoint slides and certificate of achievement. *Is This the Night* is a conversation, a sharing of life experience – this is what I did to fight against the fear that controlled my body, mind and soul and it really helped me to find a long lasting inner peace even in the midst of the emotional chaos and storms that may be swirling around me.

But make no mistake, as so many of us know, changing attitudes and actions can be hard work.

Are you ready?

Why Now? – the Journey

(from 2015)

This retreat workshop is based on decades of personal experience woven into centuries of wisdom shared by others. Sometimes we can "hear" or "see" the guidance given when presented in a slightly different way. It's a phenomenon those of us who mentor experience often. After days, weeks, months and even years of trying to get a point across, the person we're mentoring dashes up and says, *"You won't believe what I just heard!"*

So I learned long ago to stop worrying about who carried that message of hope, but to keep my gratitude focused on the fact that the message was delivered…and accepted.

As a battered woman, I experienced the full weight of Society's prejudice and discrimination – ***What did you do to cause this***? In the early eighties, it was rare to find another person to talk to who truly knew how I felt. I know that isolation. I don't live there anymore. I found inner peace and with that peace, freedom from fear. And living free from fear opened the door of opportunity to be fully a-part-of life…

So, after all these years, now that I ease on down a spiritually based path in some degree of inner peace each day, why bring this all up again now? **Why now**? Because I became aware of another group of people who like me and my mother before me, and millions before her – are sitting in silence, paralyzed with fear

"What did you do to cause it?"

It took a long time to erase that irrational sense of guilt from my entire being.

As a former battered woman has much changed in 33 years? You decide. This is a typical experience today:

"You don't drive? Why not?"

I'm person with a visually impairment. I have no peripheral vision.

"How did that happen?"

Damage to my optic nerves, blows to the head.

"Were you in an accident?"

No, I was beaten repeatedly during my marriage…and then it begins. The jaw drops in disbelief. The eyes get wide. And then the look – pity, horror, revulsion – it all wraps into confusion. Some people even take a step or two backwards as if "it" might be contagious. It's a struggle for so many to process and I know what the thought process is (because I've been told outright):

Annemarie. Not you! You're a community activist. You're a leader. You're the rock of Gibraltar. You're so intelligent. You're always upbeat, positive, happy! You're our go-to person for everything!!!

Yes, me – Annemarie. Because battering, domestic violence, can happen to anyone.

Just like suicidal thoughts, behaviors, attempts and suicides can happen to anyone.

Yet when a person states that – *"I am a suicide attempt survivor"* or *"She died by suicide,"* the reaction from others is all too often exactly what I have experienced – the pity, shock, dismay, judgment…tongue-tied embarrassment.

Hell, I see that reaction when people ask me what I do professionally – I'm a consultant, advocate and trainer for suicide prevention, intervention, and postvention. That typically stops the conversation on a dime. I rarely hear any follow up questions. OK, so once in a while someone says, *"Oh, yes, that's really needed,"* half-heartedly. And every once in a while someone does respond with passion – *"Wow! That's awesome!"* Sadly, prejudice and discrimination is still very much alive and destructive.

And that's "Why *Now*?" This is long overdue.

And that explains what I see as the thin, but common thread that weaves between domestic violence/PTSD and the similar emotional chaos thrashing inside anyone impacted by a suicide attempt or loss. Prejudice and discrimination breeds irrational shame, irrational blame, irrational guilt (What did *I* do wrong?) – and yet, we stay silent.

After I regained consciousness from my first brutal beating, my first thought was not to call anyone for help, my first thought would set the course of my life for the next 17 years; *I wonder what I did wrong & whatever it was, I'll fix it.* " It's not uncommon for the loved one of an attempt survivor to feel this way – how can *I* fix this? The truth was, I did nothing wrong. The truth is, as family and friends of suicide attempt survivors, we cannot "fix it."

I did nothing wrong. Families and friends of attempt survivors did nothing wrong. Loss survivors did nothing wrong. It took time and practice to slowly step away from the negative self-talk, but it can be done. It's never been about right and wrong.

Now the last thing the world needs is another 12th Step group – there are more than 200 already; however, some of the process used within the 12th-step modality can be helpful.

What follows in this retreat workshop is a little bit self-inventory, a little bit meditation exercise, a lot of writing (or maybe just some). It's sprinkled with honesty, learned and lived experience, irreverence and humor, and sometimes tears. Most of all, it's about hope.

The ultimate goal (we grant writers can't help ourselves. Everything we write, even the shopping list, must have goals and outcomes) – the goal is to be free, to have freedom from fear, blame, judgment, anger, controlling behavior – and to find some peace within.

We are imperfect beings and that's a good thing.

Why Now? – the Professional

(from October 2013)

"And what do I say to the families of attempt survivors?"

The question was peppered with anger. Perhaps it was her passion and concern, but to me, it felt angry. The question was interjected into a conference call in late 2013, in discussion about our upcoming suicide prevention conference in April of 2014. We had just voted to invite a suicide attempt survivor to be our second day keynote speaker.

We were in locations across the state, not face to face, but the discomfort was tangible. The person challenging us was concerned about the day to day, paralyzing fear so many family members of attempt survivors endure. We had no quick fix. We had nothing to which we could refer her. There really were no resources. And that was and *is* a major problem.

As I hung up from the call, I knew she had identified a huge gap in services and that just stuck with me. A couple of weeks later, at a curriculum training, I approached my boss about my discomfort. I shared that I knew what she meant about that fear. It had once owned me. A bit tongue in cheek, I noted that the world did not need another twelfth-step program…but perhaps we could learn from them.

He smiled. You know the smile. The one that confirms your concern and also implies that you are completely free to pursue that concern...without a budget, of course.

At the time, I was in the midst of producing a documentary about suicide attempt survivors, *A Voice at the Table*. It was impossible to ignore the nagging questions. What can we do to help support the friends and families of suicide attempt survivors – people who are emotionally drained and exhausted, worried about the loved ones – will there be yet another attempt? It's an insidious, often unspoken fear.

It's a common concern. Families of recovering alcoholics and drug addicts experience the same fear. Families of our military, active duty or returning veterans with post-traumatic stress and depression, experience the same fear. Victims of domestic abuse experience the same fear. It's a fear I know too well.

64

When I shared my concerns with a friend, the push back was – well, what did you do, Annemarie, to break the chains of fear? Shouldn't you share that with this group (friends/family of suicide attempt survivors)?

So I did.

In this retreat workshop format.

The Author

Annemarie Matulis, a survivor of childhood trauma and domestic violence, ha[...]
in the public, private and non-profit sectors including domestic violence, sub[...]
prevention.

In 2008, she founded a teen center for youth at risk in Taunton MA and [...]
Weekend News/Paul Newman Foundation and the National Make a Diffe[...]
was one of five recipients of the Massachusetts Suicide Prevention Leadership Awa[...]
was voted "Person of the Year" in the Greater Taunton area. In 2009 she founded the Greater [...]
Prevention Task Force and in 2012, stepped up to establish the Bristol County Regional Coalition for Sui[...]
Prevention under the auspices of the Massachusetts Coalition for Suicide Prevention (MCSP). In 2016, the
Taunton Daily Gazette honored her as one of the local "Women in History" for her community activism.

In 2014, Annemarie executive produced, directed and developed *A Voice at the Table* documentary,
www.avoiceatthetable.org – a call to action to invite the voice of suicide attempt survivors to the strategic
planning and treatment tables. LivingWorks Education shared the film with all of its trainers and it can be found
on the SPRC.org Web site as well as the National Suicide Prevention Lifeline's *With Help Comes Hope* Web
site's "Timeline." In August 2015, *A Voice at the Table* received "Honorable Mention" at the SAMHSA Voice
Awards.

During the development of the film, Annemarie began creating a curriculum for suicide attempt survivors titled,
Re-Energize & Re-Connect Suicide Attempt Survivor Workshop Program which launched in August 2015. She
also developed a retreat workshop and workbook for friends and family of suicide attempt survivors, those who
self-injure and those who struggle with suicidal thinking. *Is This the Night: Finding Inner Peace* can also be a
valuable tool for families with loved ones struggling with substance abuse as well as survivors of domestic
violence and trauma.

In 2016, Annemarie executive produced and directed the second film in the "Voices" series – *Voices Still
Unheard* – that focused on the difficult journey of teens who experienced excessive sadness, depression, self-
injury, suicidal thoughts and suicide attempts and their parents' battle with securing mental health care for them
and re-entry into schools after treatment. The third documentary in the series, *Voices from the Shadows* debuted
in 2017 and reveals the difficult journey through fear to healing experienced by family and friends of suicide
attempt survivors. The film is a companion to the workbook *Is This the Night: Finding Inner Peace.*

...ating the regional coalition, Annemarie is a consultant for the Garrett Lee Smith State &
...outh Suicide with the Massachusetts Department of Public Health, serves on the Executive
...he Massachusetts Coalition for Suicide Prevention, chairs its Social Media Committee and
...production of PSAs and the MCSP version of Ted Talks. She also sits on the board of directors of a
...profit, is a successful grant writer, an active member of the American Association of Suicidology, and
...gnized public speaker and author. Annemarie is a trainer for several modules of suicide prevention,
...rvention and postvention and a certified suicide loss grief support facilitator.

In December 2017, the web site devoted to the film A Voice at the Table was converted into a safe Haven,
home base for the growing Family & Friends movement. www.avoiceatthetable.org

And then there's this...

Thank you to the Friday night friends – Tracey, George, Bill, Eric, Michael, Theresa, Sue, and Peter. Much love to the Tapestry crew, my spiritual recharge – not going to try to get you all in a list. Our Kitchen Table Conversation Grief Support members for their honesty and willingness to share their experiences. And the same for the Re-Energize & Re-Connect attempt and loss survivors.

From *Voices from the Shadows*

Cara Ana
Dese'Rae L. Stage
Craig Miller
Paula Christina Sousa Paluch
Edward Paluch
Jennie Babcock
Joe Babcock
Jocelyn Figlock
Rick Strait
Holden Strait
Annemarie Matulis
Tracey Pacheco Medeiros

And to all the parents, family, and friends of those who attempted suicide, self-injure or suffer from consistent thoughts of suicide, thank you for taking the time to share your stories, your fears, and your hopes with us over the past several years.

A special Shout Out! to the entire #SPSMChat crew (way too many to name) for being so welcoming and listening to me every week say "family/friend of suicide attempt survivors."

There are far too many working to prevent suicide and promote life who have impacted me in so many good ways to mention – because I know I'll leave someone out, but I do need to mention a few: Sally Spencer Thomas, Marcia Epstein, Franklin Cook.

Jennifer Kelliher and my colleagues from the Massachusetts Coalition for Suicide Prevention and all the regional coalitions. With special thanks to Department of Public Health staff Christine Farrell O'Reilly, Alan Holmlund, Kelley Cunningham, Janice Ventre, Alison Brill, Brandy Brooks. The Garrett Lee Smith compadres, Maura Weir, Bear and Janet Mazziotti. My friends and colleagues at AFSP.

Debbie Brown and the entire Silver City Teen Center – the advisory board, volunteers and nine years of youth who trusted us just enough…everyone within the Bristol County Regional Coalition for Suicide Prevention and its community-based coalitions in Taunton (and East Taunton), New Bedford, Attleboro and Fall River.

Lynn Clifford (world's best cheerleader), Paul Boudreau and Fr. Richard Bardusch, the Greater Taunton Community Services, Inc. Board for letting me hang out. Rev. Jim Tilbe. Greg Tobin for his infinite patience, (Aunt Patty I love you).

Why all of this at the end of a workbook and some much "background" throughout? Because this didn't just happen out of thin air. It took all of this and more to put these pages together. This is not and was never intended to be a by-the-book text book. It's a compilation of lived experience.

And like we ourselves, it's not perfect, but it is a beginning.

References

National Action Alliance for Suicide Prevention: Suicide Attempt Survivors Task Force. (2014). *The Way Forward: Pathways to hope, recovery, and wellness with insights from lived experience*. Washington, DC.

Cameron, J. (2002). *The artist's way: A spiritual path to higher creativity*, New York: J.P. Tarcher/Putnam.

Resources:

www.avoiceatthetable.org

https://www.facebook.com/Is-This-the-Night-125437314912158/

http://www.suicidology.org

http://livethroughthis.org

http://www.masspreventssuicide.org/

https://www.facebook.com/annemarie.matulis

https://www.facebook.com/SuicidePreventionBristolCounty/

https://smile.amazon.com/dp/0997423951/ref=sr_1_3?ie=UTF8&qid=1492045738&sr=8-3&keywords=embracing+imperfection

If you or anyone you know is at risk and needs help, call:
1-800-273-8255 (TALK)
Push 1 for veterans

https://suicidepreventionlifeline.org

Crisis Text Line: 741741

https://www.facebook.com/spsmchat/

www.afsp.org

https://www.thetrevorproject.org

https://www.translifeline.org/

Made in the USA
Columbia, SC
26 September 2021